Buzz off,
Bill
Tess
Bill
Jill
Emma
Jeff
Don
Meg

I will tell Miss Hill!

Miss! Miss! Bill has got my hat.
Miss Hill

Buzz off, Bill!

Miss! Miss! Bill has got my pen.

Buzz off, Bill!

Miss! Miss! Bill has got the ball.

Buzz off, Bill!

Miss! Miss! Bill has got my pot.

Buzz off, Bill!

Miss! Miss! Bill is in a mess!

Brrrrrrrrrrr!
Yes! The bell!

Miss Hill gets on the bus.

Miss Hill gets off the bus.

Buzz off, Ross!

Mum! Mum! Ross has got my doll!